P9-DGP-847

TODAY'S GOSPEL

TODAY'S GOSPEL

AUTHENTIC OR SYNTHETIC?

Walter J. Chantry

THE BANNER OF TRUTH TRUST

THE BANNER OF TRUTH TRUST
3 Murrayfield Road, Edinburgh EH12 6EL, UK
P.O. Box 621, Carlisle, PA 17013, USA

*

© The Banner of Truth Trust 1970
First published 1970
Reprinted 1971
Reprinted 1972
Reprinted 1972
Reprinted 1975
Reprinted 1976
Reprinted 1980
Reprinted 1982
Reprinted 1985
Reprinted 1989
Reprinted 1997
Reprinted 2001
Reprinted 2006
Reprinted 2008
Reprinted 2009

ISBN: 978 0 85151 027 9

*

Typeset in 10.5/15 pt Sabon Oldstyle at
The Banner of Truth Trust, Edinburgh

Printed in the USA by
Versa Press, Inc.
East Peoria, IL

*

ACKNOWLEDGMENTS

There are three men who have been of considerable help to me in producing this book. I would like gratefully to acknowledge their kind labour and counsel. They are:

A carpenter, who has been my spiritual father and principal teacher in the faith;

A merchant, who has faithfully shared the oversight of our local church throughout my brief ministry;

An Arab, whose love for Christ and spiritual fellowship has immensely enlarged the joy of my sojourn.

Contents

What's Wrong with Evangelism Today?

Truth and unity

Evangelicals know that all is not well in their churches and missions. Behind the facade of glowing missionary reports and massive statistics there is a profound awareness that the church has little power in evangelism. While bravely trying to produce an aura of joy and victory among their followers, church leaders are uneasy and deeply dissatisfied with their present experience and the results of their efforts.

The church is astir with questions about evangelism and hope for revival. Never have there been more missionaries. Never have there been more evangelistic campaigns. Never were more Christians studying to do personal evangelism. Never were there such enormous conferences to examine seriously the causes and cure of lameness in the gospel ministry.

In 1966, 165 mission agencies and fifty-five schools convened at Wheaton, Illinois in a Congress on the church's worldwide mission. Their task was to address themselves to the barriers preventing success in a world evangelistic thrust. Soon after that, 1300 men of 100 nations met in Berlin. They fervently hoped that this Congress on Evangelism would 'light the fuse for a worldwide evangelistic explosion.' In 1969 great numbers met at St Louis to investigate and stimulate evangelism. Other such gatherings are to be expected in the future.

Yet the bewilderment is deepening among missionaries and local churches. After analysing, evaluating, praying and hoping, missions are not revitalized and sinners are not turning to Christ in great numbers. The questions are still being asked, 'What's wrong with our evangelism? What is needed to win the world for Christ? Where is the power of Edwards and Whitefield?'

In this honest search for God's power to return to the preaching of today, evangelicals have been making some crucial errors. Those who believe in God's Word have been grasping at the same superficial solutions that liberalism has adopted. Relevance, respectability (whether intellectual or social), and especially unity have become the aims of God's people with the hope that these will revitalize a weakened church.

'If only all Bible-believing people join together, the world will sit up and listen,' thinks the church. Let's merge our mission boards to pool our funds and our personnel. Let's join giant evangelistic projects. If every evangelical joins in a common organization, we can have greater depth of evangelism. Thus organizational unity becomes the aim of gospel churches.

Having accepted the theory that unity is all-important for world evangelism, both the church and the individual must lower their estimate of the value of truth. In a large congress on evangelism we could not insist on a truth of God's Word that would offend *any* brother evangelical. Thus we must find the lowest common denominator to which all born-again Christians hold. The rest of the Bible will be labelled 'unessential' for missions. After all, unity (among Christians) is more essential than doctrinal preciseness.

It is for just this reason that the mission societies have been unwilling carefully to examine the root problem in preaching. Mission boards are hesitant to answer the question, 'What is the gospel?' Thoroughly to answer that would condemn what many of their own missionaries preach. It would destroy the mission society, which is a federation of churches who have differing answers to that question. To adopt the position of one church would be to lose the support of five others. The whole system built on unity and generality would crumble.

The local church may not get too specific about truth either. It may affect its harmony with the denomination or association. To define the gospel carefully will bring conflict with the organizations working with teenagers. It will prompt irritating problems with mission boards and embarrassing disagreement with missionaries supported for years. It may condemn the whole Sunday School programme. Giving too much attention to the content of the gospel will mean friction with other evangelicals. And unity is the key to success.

Tradition in evangelism

Evangelicals cherish their Reformation heritage. We stand in the line of Luther and others who have broken the back of papal superstitions. The Bible, God's Holy Word, is our guide in all things. We bow to no human authority.

Such a claim flows from a right spirit of supreme allegiance to God. Yet the cry 'Sola Scriptura' is more often an indication of good intention than it is fact. The evangelical wing of the Protestant church is saturated with doctrine and practices which have no biblical foundation. Many teachings and habits touching the gospel are as much the products of human invention and tradition as were the indulgences of Tetzel. And certain doctrines in our midst are quite as dangerous.

In the central issue of the way of salvation, large segments of Protestantism are engrossed in neo-traditionalism. We have inherited a system of evangelistic preaching which is unbiblical. Nor is this tradition very ancient. Our message and manner of preaching the gospel cannot be traced back to the Reformers and their creeds. They are much more recent innovations. Worse, they cannot be traced to the Scriptures. They have clearly arisen from superficial exegesis and a careless mixture of twentieth-century reason with God's revelation.

The resulting product is a dangerous conglomerate—just the sort that Satan uses to delude the souls of sinners. What cult has not learned to use verses of the Bible and half truths to establish their lies? That has been the devil's strategy from the beginning [*Gen.* 3:5]. By selling another gospel to our generation, Satan has been employing many sincere men in preaching a dethroned Christ. The glories of the Saviour are being hidden even from his servants because preachers will not give careful attention to the gospel of God's Word alone.

Products of modern evangelism are often sad examples of Christianity. They make a profession of faith, and then continue to live like the world. 'Decisions[1] for Christ' mean very little. Only a small proportion of those who 'make decisions' evidence the grace of God in a transformed life. When the excitement of the latest campaign has subsided, when the choir sings no more thrilling choruses, when large crowds no longer gather, when the emotional hope in the evangelist's 'invitation' has moved

---

1 To become a Christian, a sinner must decide to turn from sin and trust the Saviour. Repentance and faith are inward acts of the human will. But these must be carefully distinguished from the outward procedure of going forward, verbally confessing sin and publicly asking Christ to be one's Saviour. In this paper the term 'decision' will refer to the formal ceremonies connected with evangelistic services; for these have become identified with 'decisions' in the evangelical mind, with the unfounded assumption that participants in outward ceremonies have inwardly decided to follow Christ.

to another city, what do we have that is real and lasting? When every house in our mission village has been visited, what has been done? The honest heart answers, 'Very little.' There has been a great deal of noise and dramatic excitement, but God has not come down with his frightful power and converting grace.

All of this is related to the use of a message in evangelism that is unbiblical. The truth necessary for life has been hidden in a smoke screen of human inventions. On the shallow ground of man's logic, large numbers have been led to assume they have a right to everlasting life and have been given an assurance which does not belong to them. Evangelicals are swelling the ranks of the deluded with a perverted gospel. Many who have 'made decisions' in modern churches and been told in the inquiry rooms that their sins have been forgiven, will be as surprised as Tetzel's customers to hear, 'I never knew you; depart from me' [*Matt.* 7 :23].

Many of you who read these pages have inherited practices and teachings which you have assumed to be the right way of evangelism. You have never seen a lively church actively evangelize in any other way, so you have never questioned it. I know that there are some who claim to possess a more precise theology of evangelism who do nothing to win sinners to Christ. Absence of evangelistic zeal is a dreadful predicament on one hand. But there is also the danger of zeal which is not according to knowledge. Could you be misleading souls and misdirecting the labours of other Christians? Have you closely examined your message and methods in the light of God's Word?

Pastors, this is no idle question. Have you not wondered about those 'converts' who are as carnal as ever? What about those who have 'decided for Christ' and you cannot tell what they decided? They are not godly like the Saviour they profess, nor zealous for his cause. They do not study the Word and do not mind if they are absent when it is preached. Consequently, you know that they give no evidence of true conversion. Have you considered the possibility that they were never evangelized at all? Have your preaching and methods led them to comfort apart from Christ?

Unless our churches rethink the way of salvation by an honest search of God's Word, evangelical Protestantism will be choked in the morass of human tradition, as was Rome years ago. Already many of its members are shackled as sadly as the ignorant subjects of the Pope. Unity must not be sought at the expense of the gospel.

Many case histories of our Lord's personal evangelism and many apostolic sermons would serve well for defining the gospel. Jesus' interview with the rich young ruler has been chosen because it is a vivid instance of the elements essential to gospel preaching which are found everywhere in the New Testament. The words of Mark 10:17-27 stand in stark contrast with the prevailing doctrine of evangelicals today. The difference between today's gospel and Jesus' gospel are not in minor details, but in the core of the matter. Modern changes are serious enough to grieve the Spirit and yield empty nets. They are dangerous enough to misguide souls for eternity.

Some will immediately retreat behind the convenient shield of relativism. The excuse, 'It's only a matter of emphasis,' will be used to escape a serious self-examination in the light of God's Word. But the ensuing contrasts between Christ's gospel and today's popularized 'gospel' are crucial, not peripheral. In these contrasting messages may lie the difference between life and death for a soul, between vitality and sterility for a church.

No sincere Christian intends to deceive sinners. In love for souls, true evangelicals invariably present some profound truths in their witnessing. Yet by the unconscious omission of essential ingredients of the gospel, many fail to communicate even that portion of God's Word which they mean to convey. When a half truth is presented as the whole truth, it becomes an untruth.

Though the answers may be painful, you must ask if your church, your missionaries, your evangelists, your Sunday School teachers, and you, yourself, are preaching our Lord's gospel. Though the answer may bring discomfort, conflict, misunderstanding, and loss of friends, you cannot dishonour God by ignoring his truth. If you are unwilling to take a firm stand on the content of the gospel, then say no more about zeal, sacrifice and activity. If you are not willing to insist that the 'story to tell to the nations' be precisely Jesus' story, why go on with 'evangelism' and 'missions' at all?

Look closely then at the Master Evangelist of all ages. Listen to his message, observe his motives, and note his methods. Then reflect on your own ministry. In the young man of 30 AD you will see the faces of young men of 1970. To reach them, you must say what our Lord said. To please God you must labour as Christ laboured. Cast off the shackles of evangelical traditions! Refuse to pay for outward unity with the coins of fundamental truth. Learn to follow the Christ of the Scriptures in evangelism. Lay hold of the authentic gospel and discard the synthetic.

1

Preaching the Character of God

And when he was gone forth into the way, there came one running, and kneeled to him, and asked him, Good Master, what shall I do that I may inherit eternal life? And Jesus said unto him, Why callest thou me good? there is none good but one, that is, God.

[Mark 10:17,18]

The rich young ruler's assets

A glance at the young man who came to Jesus indicates that he was a person worthy of your esteem and confidence. He was a 'cleancut' youth. He greeted our Lord with abundant courtesy: 'kneeled to him' and called Him, 'Good Master'. His deep interest in religion must command your respect. He 'came running' to Christ in enthusiastic pursuit of spiritual help. So anxious was he to secure 'eternal life' that he could not wait for a private conversation. On the highway he ignored the public's attention to inquire after his soul's welfare.

Further, he was a man of moral action. When Jesus began to remind him of the commandments, he responded, 'All these have I observed from my youth' [verse 20]. His life was visibly pure. When Jesus said, 'Do not commit adultery', he could sincerely report that he had been chaste. To our Lord's command, 'Do not steal,' he could say that he was honest in business. His wealth was not gained by fraud. He had always respected his parents. He was no slanderer. Such integrity was not occasional or newly acquired. Rather, morality had been woven into his habits 'from his youth.'

Verse 22 tells us that the fellow 'had great possessions.' He was successful in the world. Luke 18:18 calls him a 'ruler' - a nobleman of authority and influence. Matthew 19:20 says he was a 'young man,' which makes his accomplishments more surprising. 'A worthy candidate for the Citizen of the Year Award', you might think. And certainly you would love to have him as a trophy for Christ. You would be delighted to see him confess Jesus and join your church. Isn't it a shame that part of your interest in such a person would stem from the carnal suspicion that one so successful in the world would enhance God's kingdom on earth?

What would be your reflex to such a circumstance? Here is an outstanding fellow begging to know how he can get to heaven! This is the evangelist's dream! Wouldn't you open your Bible and ask him essential questions? 'Do you believe that you are a sinner? Do you believe that Christ died for sinners? Will you accept Jesus as your personal Saviour? Pray this prayer after me . . . .' He would answer in the affirmative to each question with very little instruction. Just show him the usual verses. This rich man was ripe for our evangelism. Our inquiry rooms would have elicited his 'decision' in a few moments, and given him assurance of eternal life besides. He would be added to the statistic sheet and his conversion reported across the world. Such a celebrity might even merit a personal write-up in the big evangelical magazines!

Aren't you a little disappointed to see Jesus handling this tender soul so roughly? How could our Lord use such obviously poor tactics with a sinner? He began with a rebuke, went on to talk about the Ten Commandments (of all things!), demanded immense sacrifice as a condition of having eternal life, and allowed the 'fish' to get away! Didn't he know how to lead a soul to himself? If you are surprised, surely you are the one who doesn't understand evangelism. Look again.

Jesus' rebuke

Jesus addressed his first response, not to the ruler's question, but to the incidental greeting given to him. The young man had called Jesus 'Good Master'. But our Lord refused to accept the compliment. The inquirer was only aware that Jesus was a great teacher. He was ignorant that he was speaking to the Christ, the Son of the living God. The Saviour took this opportunity to say in effect, 'The goodness of any creature (and such only, you take me to be) is not worthy to be named or taken notice of. It is God alone who is originally and essentially good.'[1]

It is true that we should not lavish our most glorious adjectives upon men. For then what words will we use to praise our God? But did Jesus have to take the young fellow so literally? Can't we use the term 'good' to refer courteously or generally to men? Does the Lord expect us to interrupt every conversation literally to correct all plaudits given to fellow-creatures? What is Christ's purpose for insisting on this minor point?

The Great Evangelist was not being petty. Nor does he expect us to campaign against using the word 'good' to describe men. Our Master himself labelled righteous men 'good' [*Matt.* 5:45]. However, this was not an ordinary conversation but a very intense one. Jesus was rebuking the man for having a readiness to flatter men but little reverence toward God. At the outset of the discussion he wished to honour God and stir a respect for his holy character. So he seized upon the seeker's salutation as an occasion for instruction. Jesus began his message of evangelism by solemnly fixing attention on God's attribute of infinite holiness or goodness.

Jesus' motive

Our Lord was motivated in his conversation by love and compassion for the covetous youth. Verse 21 states ex-

1 Henry Scougal, *The Life of God in the Soul of Man*, Inter-Varsity Press, 1961, p 31.

plicitly that Jesus had a conscious love for the man as he talked with him. When the youth departed from Jesus, because he could not save his soul and his money too, there must have been the gnawing pain of pitying sorrow in our Lord's heart. He wept to see Jerusalem refuse his offers of mercy. Similar emotion for this particular sinner was likely felt as he turned away. The man was not merely a hopeful statistic, nor a trophy of success to embellish his crusade reports. Jesus deeply loved the ruler. Such love for sinners is an essential qualification for any evangelist.

However, concern for the nobleman's soul was not the supreme motive that moved Christ to witness to this sinner. Running even deeper within his breast was a love of God. Though induced by a desire to save men, Christ was primarily motivated by a longing to glorify his Father. You cannot carefully read the Gospels and fail to see that our Lord's chief aim in every act was to do the will of his Father and to make his glory known to men.

Upon humbling himself to enter this world Christ said, 'Lo, I come to do thy will, O God' [*Heb.* 10:7]. In life he reported, 'I do always those things that please him' [*John* 8:29].

As he went to the cross, Jesus summarized his ministry thus: 'I have glorified thee on the earth: I have finished the work which thou gavest me to do' [*John* 17:4]. This burning passion consumed him throughout his life.

An evangelist of today must know what it is to be committed above all else to glorifying God. Some who demonstrate a passion for accurate doctrine, place a question mark over their love for God by evidencing no active love for lost sinners. This absence of missionary effort is appalling. Nevertheless, if being moved by compassion for sinners is essential, it is more essential to be moved more profoundly still by a love of God.

Jesus' message

Such motivation and determination will display itself in the evangelist's message. The questioner in this passage had centred attention upon his own need (of finding a way to inherit eternal life). Jesus, however, turned the primary focus of the interview upon God and his glory. His entire message was structured to honour his Father. The man wanted a solution to his fear of death and judgment. Jesus would eventually address himself with compassion to this concern, but first a foundation had to be laid and a more important issue settled. Jesus' answer indicated that he had come to exalt Jehovah, to declare his name, to tell of his unique goodness. His coming to save men was rooted in this.

Evangelism always requires preaching on the attributes of God. When Jesus met the Samaritan woman at Jacob's well [*John* 4], he taught her that God is a Spirit. When Paul addressed the heathen on Mars' Hill [*Acts* 17], he had to devote even more of his evangelistic message to the character of God, who was unknown to them. He began by speaking of God as the Creator, as the Sustainer of all life, as the Mighty One who raised Jesus from the dead. This element, of exalting God's character, is essential to bringing honour to God in our preaching.

Much of modern preaching is anæmic, with the life-blood of God's nature absent from the message. Evangelists centre their message upon man. Man has sinned and missed a great blessing. If man wants to retrieve his immense loss he must act thus and so. But the gospel of Christ is very different. It begins with God and his glory. It tells men that they have offended a holy God, who will by no means pass by sin. It reminds sinners that the only hope of salvation is to be found in the grace and power of this same God. Christ's gospel sends men to beg pardon of the Holy One.

There is a wide difference between these two messages. The one seeks to blaze a trail to heaven for man while ignoring the Lord of Glory. The other labours to magnify the God of all grace in the salvation of men. The first would give a technical answer to, 'What shall I do to inherit eternal life?', 'without an adequate foundation. The last says,

> Wait a moment. The God with whom we have to do is thrice holy, alone good, unapproachable in brilliant holiness! We will return to your question in its subordinate

place. But now take your eye from yourself and behold the holy God of the Scriptures. Then you will see yourself as you truly are—a creature in rebellion against an infinitely pure God. You are not yet prepared to discuss yourself and eternity.

This does not mean that preaching about the character of God is isolated from seeking the salvation of a sinner. Preaching on the attributes is essential to the conversion of a man. Without a knowledge of God, a sinner does not know whom he has offended, who threatens him with destruction, or who is able to save him. Apart from some clear apprehensions of God, there can be no personal approach to God, and 'personal Saviour' becomes a hollow phrase.

Jesus lifted the egocentric eyes of the wealthy ruler to One whose holiness caused Isaiah to cry, 'Woe is me! for I am undone' [*Isa.* 6:5]. Is that a secondary part of the gospel? If you think so, you don't understand the first things of the faith. The rich youth had come running because he understood that he might not inherit eternal life. But he didn't understand why. Whom had he offended? There was no remorse for having offended a holy God. He was prepared to talk of religion; but he was ignorant of God. He was anxious to ask for the joys of salvation; but he could not confess as David, 'Against thee, thee only, have I sinned; and done this evil in thy sight' [*Psa.* 51 :4]. He was not acquainted with the Lord.

When Saul was arrested by a shining light on the road to Damascus, a voice demanded, 'Saul, Saul, why persecutest thou me?' [*Acts* 9:4]. Immediately Saul asked, 'Who art thou?'. Whom have I persecuted? How is that? The one who came running to Jesus had the same question, for he had never seen the transcendent holiness of God. Ignorant of Jehovah's unspeakable dignity, he was unaware of the enormity of his crime. Though he had not loved the Lord with all his heart, the youth did not conceive of this as criminal neglect, because he had never beheld the glory of God. He was unready to hear of the way of salvation.

Although the inquirer was a Jew, and probably devout, Jesus did not assume that he knew who God was. He needed catechizing on the attributes of God. Evangelists today are making the dreadful miscalculation that sinners know who God is. The sad truth is that *our* age knows less than the Jews of our Lord's day. Nevertheless, evangelicals plunge right in with 'five things God wants you to know.' They all centre upon the man's eternal fortunes and utterly ignore the question, 'Who is God?'. The sinners thus treated never realize the gravity of their plight. They don't know whom they have offended. This is tragic.

Jesus spoke to the man of God's holiness because it showed him what great trouble had come upon him. It is the invariably pure God who is your judge. The note of holiness was particularly pertinent to bringing a proper fear of God into this fellow's soul. He realized before that God was a judge. Now Jesus impressed him with the holiness of that judge, a holiness that 'will by no means clear the guilty' [*Exod.* 34:7].

Today, we are told that witnessing is to begin with, 'God loves you and has a wonderful plan for your life'. Love is set before sinners as the foremost characteristic of God. But Jesus didn't begin that way. And the Bible as a whole speaks more often of God's holiness than of his love. This is probably because men readily remember all attributes that might favour themselves and totally forget those which threaten or alarm them.

Thousands of sinners think of God as having only one attribute—'love'. Though that is part of the truth, when it is taken for the whole truth it becomes a lie. When you tell a stranger, 'God loves you,' his mind registers something like this: 'Yes, he loves me and would never harm me. He loves me with forgiving and merciful kindness; so, all is well with my soul.' In the concept of the average American, there is no idea that God is holy; only a perverted concept that he has a gushy, all-embracing kindness. Modern evangelism is helping to foster this misconception of God by its silence and vagueness.

To say to a rebel, 'God loves you and has a wonderful plan for your life,' is terribly misinforming. The truth is that God is holy. Thus, he is angry with the sinner at this moment. His sword of wrath already hangs over the head of the guilty and will forever torment him unless he repents and trusts Christ. This plan is not so wonderful. God's redeeming love for sinners is found only in Christ, and the sinner is out of Christ. The modern approach is diametrically opposed to Jesus' method with the young ruler. He did not soothe him in his ignorance, but stirred up fear by preaching that God is essentially good.

Men today will readily use the name of God as would the rich man. But it is disastrous to assume that men are speaking of the same person as we are. When we say 'God' we mean 'Creator'. When our contemporaries say 'God' they are often speaking of one who has little to do with the world we see. When we say 'God' we mean 'One who is sovereign in creation, providence, and in the redemption of his creature, man.' When sinners say 'God' they usually refer to one who has committed himself to honouring the sovereign will of man at any cost to himself. Above all, when we say 'God' we speak of One who has unflinching holiness, 'Who will by no means clear the guilty.' Sinners frequently think of 'God' as flexible so that he will by no means punish wonderful men.

Do you declare in your witnessing that God is holy? Every part of your message rests upon the character of God. If you rush into four easy steps to heaven with a man who has a defective view of God, you will deceive him and yourself. You may lead him to pray after you, and you will be praying to the God of glorious holiness. But when he repeats 'God' in his prayer, he will be praying to another god, or at best to his 'unknown god'.

'How shall they believe on him of whom they have not heard?' [*Rom.* 10:14] is a pertinent question for today's evangelist. Sinners must know him upon whom they must call to be saved. 'Salvation is of the Lord' [*Jon.* 2:9]. His power and his grace alone can deliver from destruction and lead to eternal life. Eliminating the doctrine of God from evangelism is no innocent shift in emphasis, but is cutting the heart out of our message.

'What must I do to inherit eternal life?' asked the religious youth. You must apply to Jehovah for it. But before you rush into his courts, let me tell you that he is so holy that if one ray of his glory were to meet your eye, you would be cast at his feet with a dreadful sense of uncleanness. He is a consuming fire, and you must cry out to him for mercy. Do not think that you do him a favour by 'accepting Jesus'? The Holy One has done you a great favour in commanding you to trust his Son.

Preaching several easy steps to heaven is not evangelism. Preaching the whole counsel of God is. Preaching the radiant truth of the unique goodness of God especially is. Telling men that God is their Creator may embarrass you with intellectual evolutionists, but it is essential to the gospel. Telling men that God is holy, wise and sovereign is also vital. These are not unnecessary trappings.

Someone no doubt objects:

My mission board calls such doctrines 'unessential' because they are divisive. Serious conflict would arise if I suggested that dwelling only on the love of God misleads sinners. And the pressure to get results doesn't allow time for such preaching.

Where did any group of theologians or administrators get the audacity to relegate the character of God to the category of the unessential? When liberals said that the virgin birth was an unnecessary truth, men left their churches and schools in droves. If 'evangelicals' say that the holiness and sovereignty of God are subjects too sensitive to preach, perhaps it is time to instruct others boldly at all costs, even though it involves conflict and exclusion from their fellowship.

Paul was a missionary evangelist, not a settled pastor. He could say to the Ephesian elders 'I am pure from the blood of all men' [*Acts* 20:26]. How could Paul make such a claim? Not because he had given each person four spiritual laws. That was not the New Testament method of evangelism. The next verse substantiates his claim. 'For I have not shunned to declare unto you all the counsel of God.' In his itinerant ministry Paul preached a thoroughgoing theology, not a denuded four steps to eternal life.

Today mission boards are asking their missionaries to keep the blood of men on their hands:

Don't rock the boat by clearly teaching anything that another evangelical will object to, even if it is in the Bible. Don't cause trouble by demanding the clear notes of the gospel from those who labour by your side as fellow-missionaries. Stick to the main issues.

If someone cheapens the gospel by boiling it down to a five-minute sales pitch, that is fine. If another insists upon preaching the attributes of God, that is doctrinaire. Surely something is gravely amiss in the church.

It is time to break with the neo-traditionalism of the evangelical world. The mass of poor dying sinners need preaching like Christ's. The world perishes for lack of a God-exalting declaration of his nature. Let us follow Jesus' example with the rich young ruler.

2

Preaching the Law of God

Thou knowest the commandments, Do not commit adultery, Do not kill, Do not steal, Do not bear false witness, Defraud not, Honour thy father and mother. And he answered and said unto him, Master, all these have I observed from my youth. Then Jesus beholding him loved him, and said unto him, One thing thou lackest: go thy way, sell whatsoever thou hast, and give to the poor.

[Mark 10:19-21a]

First nine commandments

The more closely we analyse our Lord's message to the rich sinner, the more striking becomes the contrast with modern evangelism. After mentioning the holiness of God, Jesus spent most of the remainder of the interview talking about God's holy law,[1] especially as summarized in the Ten Commandments.

In a sense his first remark to the young man was related to the perfect law of God. The moral law reveals the character of God. A distorted knowledge of God had kept the inquirer from adequately worshipping according to the first four commandments. He seemed to be more ready to praise men than God. Jesus' rebuke

1 All references to God's law in this chapter have in view only his moral law, which is eternal. Ceremonial and civic laws are not under consideration.

25

should have convicted the ruler of breaking the 'first table of the law.'

Our Lord went on with an explicit quotation of the next five commandments, although not in their exact order. Doesn't this seem to be an odd answer to 'What shall I do to inherit eternal life?' Surely Jesus didn't imagine that this fellow could have eternal life by keeping the law. 'A man is not justified by the works of the law, but by the faith of Jesus Christ . . . for by the works of the law shall NO flesh be justified' [*Gal.* 2:16]. Why didn't Jesus speak of the free gift offered to all? That's it! Why not offer himself as a 'personal Saviour?' Why all this attention to the law?

Again, we need to be reminded that Jesus is a better evangelist than any of us! Begin to judge your message by his, not vice versa. God's law is an *essential* ingredient of gospel preaching, for 'by the law is the knowledge of sin' [*Rom.* 3:20]. The absence of God's holy law from modern preaching is perhaps as responsible as any other factor for the evangelistic impotence of our churches and missions.

The ruler was perplexed. He had no idea what was lacking to receive eternal life. Whom had he offended? What had he done to offend God? As Jesus listed the commandments, the gentleman sincerely acquitted himself of all guilt before them. Jesus said, 'Do not commit adultery.' The rich man said, 'Completely innocent.' And so, on it went. Thus Jesus continued to press the law on him until his blinded eyes would begin to see, really see, his sin. Only by the light of the law can the vermin of sin in the heart be exposed.

After all, what is sin? The Bible's answer is found in 1 John 3:4; 'Whosoever committeth sin transgresseth also the law; for sin is the transgression of the law.' The word 'sin' makes no sense apart from God's righteous law. How could the young ruler understand his sinfulness if he completely misunderstood God's law? How can today's sinners, who are totally ignorant of God's holy law and its demands upon them, look at themselves as condemned sinners? The idea of sin is strange because God's law is foreign to their minds.

Normal evangelical practice is swiftly to run to the cross of Christ. But the cross means nothing apart from the law. Our Lord's wretched suffering must be tragic and senseless in the eyes of any who have no reverent esteem for the perfect commandments. On the cross Jesus was satisfying the just demands of the law against sinners. If sinners are unaware of the decalogue's requirements for themselves, they will see no personal significance in Christ's broken body and shed blood. Without knowledge of the condemnation of God's holy law, the cross will draw sympathy but not saving faith from sinners. Christ was set forth to be a propitiation [*Rom.* 3:25]— that is, the substitutionary object of God's wrath poured out against a violated law.

What sense was there in offering the man salvation when he had only a very vague awareness of danger? Though he had doubts that he would inherit eternal life, he certainly did not think of himself as a lawbreaker. But 'sin is the transgression of the law' [*1 John* 3:4]. So he was saying in effect that he had no real sin. And Jesus 'came not to call the righteous, but sinners to repentance' [*Luke* 5:32]. Until this moralist could see his soul in the light of God's law, he was unprepared for the gospel.

Present-day preaching only pays lip service to the concept that a man must recognize himself to be a sinner before he can genuinely embrace the Saviour. The average witnessing booklet insists on the question, 'Do you believe that all men are sinners?' If there is any hesitation, you establish the point with, 'For all have sinned and come short of the glory of God' [*Rom.* 3:23]. But no definition of sin is included. There is scarcely a man alive, including the most hardened sinner, who will deny this broad statement. Anyone would answer, 'Of course I am less holy than God. No one is perfect.' The young ruler would have conceded as much. But such is hardly an acknowledgment of sin. He would still deny that he was a liar, an adulterer, a thief.

Hosts of Christians have a dreadful fear of God's law, as if it were the useless relic of a past age, the use of which in our day would keep sinners from the grace of God. Our Saviour used the law as a primary tool of evangelism.

He knew that preaching the Ten Commandments was the only way to teach a sinner his guilt and thereby stir within him a desire for God's grace.

The woman at the well must have the seventh commandment applied to her conscience or she would never be converted. This nobleman must have the law personally preached or he would dwell in constant confusion. Every true saint would have to agree with Paul, who attributed his own conversion to the agency of the law: 'I had not known sin, but by the law' [*Rom.* 7:7]. It is God's law that convicts of sin. Until its condemnation of particular evils is forcefully pressed upon a sinner, he will not flee to Christ for mercy. At best he can only ask, 'What is it that I need for eternal life?' The man who understands the law clearly knows that only God's grace can help him. What the sinner must do is beg for mercy.

The present moment of history finds more ignorance of God's law than in many previous generations. The pulpit ignores Exodus 20. Even church members despise the fourth command, 'Remember the Sabbath day.' How can the world feel guilty in the neglect of worship? Afraid of offending the dime-store theology that has no time for God's law, many preachers are silent on the very element of truth that is needed in this hour.

Satan has effectively used a very clever device to silence the law which is needed as an instrument to bring perishing men to Christ. He has suggested that the law and love are irreconcilable enemies; they are opposites. If they are in conflict, men will obviously choose love and spurn law; for no one would dare to despise love. Thus, the wicked one has declared that love is independent of law and contrary to it.

Precisely the opposite is declared by Holy Scripture. Law and love are mutually affinitive. Jesus plainly taught that the law was urging men to nothing but love. The righteous commandments may be summarized as:

> Thou shalt love the Lord thy God with all thy heart, and with all thy soul, and with all thy mind. And thou shalt love thy neighbour as thyself. On these two commandments hang all the law and the prophets.
>
> [*Matt.* 22:37-40]

The law is neither more nor less than an elucidation of the demands of love.

In the same manner our Lord defined love by reference to the law. The repetition on this point is striking. 'If ye love me, keep my commandments' [*John* 14:15]. 'He that hath my commandments and keepeth them, he it is that loveth me' [*John* 14:21]. Love cannot be expressed without the guidelines of law, and law cannot be kept spiritually except by the motivation of love.

John very clearly said, 'This is the love of God, that we keep his commandments: and his commandments are not grievous' [*1 John* 5:3]. Love makes the law enjoyable.

Anyone who loves God delights in keeping his precepts. The man who loves God cries as David, 'Make me to go in the path of thy commandments; for therein do I delight' [*Psa.* 119:35]. To the natural man, God's laws are as chains, the harsh imposition of a ruler's will. Thus the law reveals in him an absence of love for God and men. Were his heart loving, he would not find the law grievous.

Just as love makes law enjoyable, law makes love practical. Love which is unexpressed will die. 'How can I show my affections?', asks the truly loving man. God's holy commandments give the answer. They are vents for devotion to God, as 1 John 5:3 declares. They are also guides to displaying love for men, as Romans 13:8-10 so clearly asserts:

> Owe no man any thing, but to love one another: for he that loveth another hath fulfilled the law. For this, Thou shalt not commit adultery, Thou shalt not kill, Thou shalt not steal, Thou shalt not bear false witness, Thou shalt not covet; and if there be any other commandment, it is briefly comprehended in this saying, namely, Thou shalt love thy neighbour as thyself. Love worketh no ill to his neighbour: therefore love is the fulfilling of the law.

Law and love have no quarrel. The conflict arises between law and grace as a way of salvation. Law provides no pathway to life for the sinner. It slays him and drives him to God's grace as his only hope for justification. Salvation is by grace through faith only [*Eph.* 2:8].

But this is not to suggest that law is useless for evangelism. It is useless as a standard to be kept in order to gain approval before God. 'By the deeds of the law there shall no flesh be justified in his sight' [*Rom.* 3:20]. Nevertheless, Paul extensively wielded the sword of law at the outset in Romans. This he did 'that every mouth may be stopped, and all the world may become guilty before God . . . for by the law is the knowledge of sin' [*Rom.* 3:19-20].

It is essential to declare the commandments in order to show the sinner his heart of hatred toward God and enmity toward men. Only then will he flee to the grace of God in Jesus Christ to provide him with righteousness and love.

Men are not turning to Christ because they have no sense of sinning against the Lord. They are not convicted of sin because they don't know what sin is. They have no concept of sin because the law of God is not being preached. You cannot improvise a hasty sop, 'All men have sinned.' You must dwell on the subject at length. Exposit the Ten Commandments until men are slain thereby [*Rom.* 7:11]. When you see that men have been wounded by the law, then it is time to pour in the balm of gospel oil. It is the sharp needle of the law that makes way for the scarlet thread of the gospel.[2]

2 Samuel Bolton.

Tenth commandment

Our Master found the ruler's knowledge of the commandments superficial. As he mentioned a requirement, the poor deluded man confessed innocence. Exemplary outward behaviour is not the only demand of the commandments. The young man must learn that 'the law is spiritual' [*Rom.* 7:14]. Perhaps he did recognize the stringent outward rule of the law. But he failed to appreciate that the law made demands upon the thoughts and intents of the heart. Hence our Saviour would have to be the more thorough in preaching the law. He would have to use it as a probe to bring pain deep within the soul.

To any of the commandments our Lord could have added a spiritual application, as he did in his Sermon on the Mount. With 'Do not commit adultery', he could have explained, 'that whosoever looketh on a woman to lust after her hath committed adultery with her already in his heart' [*Matt.* 5:28]. He might have expanded on 'Do not kill' to include 'whosoever is angry with his brother without a cause' [*Matt.* 5:22]. But the 'Good Master' waited to put his finger on the most darling sin of the rich man's heart.

When Jesus said, 'Sell whatsoever thou hast, and give to the poor', he was preaching the tenth commandment in an applicatory fashion. Christ was using God's word, 'Thou shalt not covet,' as a knife to lance the festering sore of greed in the man's soul. The sin was invisible to

33

the human eye. It did not show its colours on the surface of the ruler's behaviour. But in all its filth and ugliness, covetousness ruled his soul. Like a dart, the law of God pierced the conscience of this youth for the first time.

Had Jesus merely said, 'Do not covet', the polite seeker would have said, 'I do not desire anyone's property or wealth. I am satisfied with my station in life.' It would not do simply to quote Exodus 20 again. Jesus translated the tenth of God's commands into a practical test by demanding that he abandon his riches. The youth loved his riches more than he loved God and his Son, and he turned away. But when he went away, he had a clear consciousness that he was a covetous sinner. He was deficient in love for God, upon which all of the law was hanging [*Matt.* 22:40].

Do you see that Jesus was not looking for intellectual assent to the fact that the young man was less holy than God? Christ wielded the sword of God's law until it made deep and painful gashes on the ruler's conscience. The Saviour did not try to argue him into agreeing that 'all have sinned'. He continued labouring with the law till the man's soul was deeply impressed that he was a rebel against a holy God and that his soul was dreadfully sold out to Satan in covetousness.

Rather than compromise the truth of God's holy law in the name of love, our Lord allowed the ruler to depart. Had Christ ignored the inviolable character of the perfect law to win this sinner to himself, he would have destroyed love; for love is bound up in the keeping of the commandments. True love will never negotiate over the truth upon which it is established.

It is imperative that preachers of today learn how to declare the spiritual law of God; for, until we learn how to wound consciences, we shall have no wounds to bind with gospel bandages. In the twentieth century the church has tried to see how little it could say and still get converts. The assumption has been that a minimal message will conserve our forces, spread the gospel farther, and, of course, preserve a unity among evangelicals. It has succeeded in spreading the truth so thinly that the world cannot see it. Four facts droned over and over have bored sinners around us and weakened the church as well.

Now is the hour to recover the full, rich gospel of Christ. We must preach the holy character of God. We must preach the eternal law of God with diligent and thorough application to our congregations. General terminology is accomplishing just what Jesus' general mention of the law would have elicited: an ignorant, unfeeling, self-exalting protest. Oh, for the studied application of the moral law to the inward man! Where are there pulpits clearly showing that God's pure law makes strict demands upon the motives, desires, feelings and attitudes of the soul? When you find them, you also discover churches with convicted sinners prepared to hear the way of salvation.

3

PREACHING REPENTANCE TOWARD GOD

Go thy way, sell whatsoever thou hast, and give to the poor, and thou shalt have treasure in heaven. [Mark 10:21a]

Jesus had prepared the rich young ruler's heart to receive the ultimatum of the gospel. He had revealed the unmatched goodness of his Father to the sinner. He had reminded him of the law and particularly applied it to the man's heart and life. Now his listener was ready to know what he must do to inherit eternal life. He must repent and believe.

By insisting that the wealthy youth sell what he had and give to the poor, the Lord was pointing out the particular sin of covetousness in his heart. But it was not an arbitrary test by which the ruler could measure the depth of his greed. It was also an essential demand of the gospel that he forsake his wealth. He must turn his back on his 'green god' to have heavenly treasures.

This is the heart of true repentance. The New Testament word translated 'repentance' means 'a change of mind.' To be saved, covetous men must turn from the all-consuming passion after wealth. Salvation would elude the successful youth who went to Jesus unless he fundamentally changed his mind.

Paul could say, 'I count all things dung that I may win Christ' [*Phil.* 3:8]. What had been valued before conversion was despised by the apostle. He had had a change of mind. Jesus was demanding in this moment that the ruler reverse all his priorities, revolutionize his philosophy of life, and turn away from the idol of his soul. When he first hurried to Jesus, he wasn't able to understand what the gospel asks of sinners who want life. But now that he was aware of a holy God and a broken law, our Lord commands the youth to repent.

Our ears have grown accustomed to hearing men told to 'accept Jesus as your personal Saviour', a form of words which is not found in Scripture. It has become an empty phrase. These may be precious words to the Christian — 'personal Saviour'. But they are wholly inadequate to instruct a sinner in the way to eternal life. They wholly ignore an essential element of the gospel, namely repentance. And that necessary ingredient of gospel preaching is swiftly fading from evangelical pulpits, though the New Testament is filled with it.

When Jesus began his public ministry, his message was, 'The time is fulfilled, and the kingdom of God is at hand: repent ye, and believe the gospel' [*Mark* 1:15]. As he met the woman at the well, his gospel insisted that she turn from adultery. Encountering Zacchaeus, Jesus turned him from thievery to philanthropy. Now the demand to the ruler is, 'Turn from your lust for riches. Repent!'

The apostles preached the same message. Those who were closest to Christ and understood his evangelism 'went out and preached that men should repent' [*Mark* 6:12]. On the day of Pentecost Peter urged pricked hearts to 'Repent, and be baptized everyone of you in the name of Jesus Christ for the remission of sins' [*Acts* 2:38]. As he preached in the temple after the lame man was healed, his gospel was again, 'Repent ye therefore, and be converted, that your sins may be blotted out' [*Acts* 3:19]. Peter was clearly obeying our Lord's great commission. The only account of that commission which records the doctrinal content of the message to be preached is Luke 24:46-47. Here Jesus insisted 'that repentance and remission of sins should be preached in his name among all nations, beginning at Jerusalem.'

Paul confronted the intellectuals of Mars' Hill by preaching, 'God now commandeth all men everywhere to repent' [*Acts* 17:30]. This was no optional note on the apostolic trumpet. It was the melody, the theme of their instructions to sinners. Merely to talk about 'accepting a personal Saviour' eliminates this crucial imperative.

In Ephesus Paul went from house to house, 'testifying both to the Jews and also to the Greeks, repentance toward God, and faith toward our Lord Jesus Christ.' Before Agrippa, Paul asserted that his mission was 'to

open their (Gentiles') eyes, and to turn them from darkness to light, and from the power of Satan unto God, that
they may receive forgiveness of sins' [*Acts* 26:18]. To the
Gentiles Paul preached 'that they should repent and turn
to God, and do works meet for repentance' [*Acts* 26:20].

Today men are properly told to confess their sins and to
ask forgiveness. But evangelists and pastors are forgetting
to tell sinners to repent. Consequently this misinformed age
imagines that it can continue in its old ways of life while
adding Jesus as a personal hell insurance for the world to
come. Treasures on earth *and* treasures in heaven. Who
could turn down that bargain! Pleasures of sin *and* joys
of eternity. That is a good deal! Sinners are not being sad-
dened, as was the young ruler, to learn that they must turn
from sin to have eternal life. Yet it is the *sine qua non* of
the gospel promises. Scripture always joins repentance and
remission of sins [cf. *Acts* 3:19, *Luke* 24:47, *Acts* 26:18
already quoted]. Repentance is necessary to forgiveness.

Confession of sin is not enough. There must also be a
full purpose of heart to turn from the former life of sin to
a new walk in righteousness. No man can serve God and
mammon [*Matt.* 6:24]. Neither will God save any man
who continues to serve mammon. To confess, 'I have
sinned in loving riches,' while intending to pursue those
same riches with continued relish is not repentance. For
salvation the ruler must be determined to forsake as well
as confess.

'He that covereth his sins shall not prosper: but whoso confesseth *and* forsaketh them shall have mercy' [*Prov.* 28:13, emphasis added]. Though sorrowful confession is an essential part of repentance, it is not the whole of it. The change of mind which issues in definite turning away from sin is the heart and soul of true repentance.

It is no wonder, however, that repentance is not being preached today. How can a man turn to a God of whom he is ignorant? How can a sinner turn from a sin to which he is blind because God's law is unknown to him? Having considered the first part of Jesus' message 'irrelevant', modern preachers must overhaul the principal requirements made of sinners.

You can easily bring sinners to a sense of remorse because they are about to perish. Criminals are always sorry that they face punishment. Get your friends thinking of life beyond the grave and you can stir up a foreboding of possible harm to themselves. Then suggest that their imperfect lives are responsible for the threat, and you have made them ready to accept Jesus as their personal deliverer from the dreaded consequences.

But at this point you could not demand that they repent. 'What do you mean?', would be your friends' question. If you tell them to confess sorrowfully, that would be simple. But you cannot ask them to turn from sins, of which they are ignorant, to an unknown God. Unaware of any particular law broken or any serious habit of sin, they would not know what to turn from. They are sorry to know that they may perish. But they are not distressed that they have offended the holy God. Indeed, they look upon sin as the inevitable slip of creatures who cannot help themselves.

Evangelists must use the moral law to reveal the glory of the God offended. Then the sinner will be ready to weep, not only because his personal safety is endangered, but also, and primarily, because he has been guilty of treason to the King of kings. 'They shall look upon me whom they have pierced and they shall mourn for him' [*Zech.* 12:10]. The heart will then be taught to sigh,

> Who was the guilty?
> Who brought this upon thee?
> Alas, my treason, Jesus, hath undone thee.
> 'Twas I, Lord Jesus, I it was denied thee:
> I crucified thee!

Johann Heermann

The holy law must search the man's life for particular sins. It must be applied spiritually to reveal the inwardness of the crime. Then, and then only, will the sinner know what in particular he is to turn from if he is to be saved.

There is little doubt that the ruler would have received today's version of the gospel joyfully. Without the requirement of repentance, he would have gladly accepted Jesus' help to get to heaven. Surely he would admit that he came short of God's glory (although he would not mean by that what Paul did in Romans 3:10-18). Surely he would accept the free gift of eternal life 'with no strings attached'. But he would not empty his hands of filthy lucre to receive the righteous Son of God. The barrier was, 'Sell whatsoever thou hast and give to the poor'. He was not ready to do *that* to get eternal life. He is willing to have Christ. He came running to him. But he is not willing to forsake mammon.

Churches are being filled with professing Christians who have never heard that Jesus demands repentance of any who seek eternal life. People flock to 'accept Jesus as a personal Saviour' without selling all. They have never been told by the preacher that there is a condition placed on having treasures in heaven—that is, repentance. So the converts of modern evangelism are often as worldly after their 'decisions' as before; for they have made a wrong decision. The covetous still cling to their riches and pleasures. Wealth and ease remain as the prevailing marks of their lives.

In a panic over this phenomenon, the evangelicals have invented the idea of 'carnal Christians.'[1] These are said

---

1 Paul's use of the term in I Corinthians 3 is much abused. He was referring to babes in Christ [*1 Cor.* 3:1] who had an area of carnal behaviour. He never suggested that they were true Christians who had failed to bow to the rule and reign of Jesus Christ. Had they not submitted to Christ as Lord at all, they would evidently not be even babes. 'He that obeyeth not the Son shall not see life; but the wrath of God abideth on him' [*John* 3:36].

to be folks who have taken the gift of eternal life without turning from sin. They have 'allowed' Jesus to be their Saviour; but they have not yet yielded their life to the Lord. Trying to patch up a faulty evangelism, the church has adopted a faulty follow-up. It defends the questionable experiences of men and women as conversion and holds out the added carrot of 'victorious life' to those who will take a second step. Well, the rich young ruler would gladly have been a 'carnal Christian'. Wouldn't he delight to be assured of eternal life while serving the devil on earth? Needless to say, the Bible knows of no such grotesque creature as one who is saved but unrepentant. No illegitimate sons will enter God's kingdom. They must have faith as their mother. But they must also have repentance as their father.

Often Christ turned crowds away by insisting that, 'Whosoever he be of you that forsaketh not all that he hath, he cannot be my disciple' [*Luke* 14:33]. He was not speaking of abundant life nor of 'victorious' giants of the faith. He demanded this turning from *everything* to himself as a condition of discipleship for everyone. The young ruler would turn from earthly riches to heavenly or he would cling to earthly riches and perish. It was imperative that he part with his sin or with the Saviour. We have no right to lower Jesus' entrance requirements for his kingdom.

Christ has not invented a different gospel for the

44

twentieth century. But the sad fact is that evangelical missionaries, churches, and literature have unconsciously scrapped the doctrine of repentance to replace it with an easy, sorrowful confession. This fundamental, indispensable foundation stone of the gospel is being ignored. If 'The word of the beginning of Christ' [*Heb.* 6:1, lit.] is discarded, what will be the end of the souls under this influence? No wonder evangelism is ineffective! The church has great cause to be disturbed. It isn't preaching Jesus' gospel!

Paul went from house to house 'testifying repentance toward God, and faith toward our Lord Jesus Christ' [*Acts* 20:21]. That was the central message when the Spirit attended the church with his power. It is time to be preaching repentance again. Men must be confronted with Christ's ultimatum to the ruler: repent or perish at the hands of a holy God whose perfect law you have criminally despised. Jettison your sin or God will cast you out of his sight. The prodigal son could not return to his father while in the embrace of harlots. Neither can you enter heaven lovingly clutching your riches.

4

Preaching Faith Toward God's Son

Come, take up the cross, and follow me. [Mark 10:21b]

Repentance and faith are conjoined twins. Where one is found, the other will not be absent. They are invariably joined in the true convert's heart. True faith always involves repentance. True repentance always has faith mixed with it. Thus, the evangelists sometimes only tell sinners to repent, sometimes only demand that they believe, sometimes mention both. Christ demanded of the ruler faith in himself as well as repentance from the dead works of sin.

The conscientious youth had a philosophy of life which placed wealth very high in the scale of values. His thinking was built upon admiration and desire of wealth. His love was fixed upon the object of riches. His will was inclined to choose any option which would enlarge or preserve his worldly estate. In commanding repentance, our Lord was urging the rich man to abandon his philosophy of life. He must rip his intelligence, emotions and will away from earthly riches or he would possess no 'treasures in heaven.'

Yet the inquirer's thoughts, desires, and allegiance could not remain in a vacuum. When the heart is swept clean, it must not be kept unoccupied, or seven devils worse than the first will fill it [*Matt.* 12:43-45]. A new doctrine must fill the mind. Another object must possess the affections. Some master must direct the will. The ruler must believe on the Lord Jesus Christ, or turning from one sin would be only a diversion to a worse one. He must have faith.

Thus we read Jesus' gracious invitation, 'Come, follow me.' God incarnate condescends tenderly to beckon a rebel who loves money more than him. 'Come'. The invitation is given to a poor sinner who has fallen 'into temptation and a snare, and into many foolish and hurtful lusts, which drown men in destruction and perdition. For the love of money is the root of all evil' [*1 Tim.* 6:9-10]. To a lawbreaker the Saviour calls, 'Come. Believe on me. Give me your mind, your love, your obedience.'

Again, it is necessary to clear up confused and erroneous ideas about faith. How was Jesus offering himself to the guilty youth? As One to be followed, that is, 'Learn from me, imitate me, obey me. You called me "Master." Now act the part of a servant and follower. I don't just want you to say that I am Master. I want you to believe it. Come, follow Me.' Thus Jesus inquired in Luke 6:46, 'Why call ye me Lord, Lord, and do not the things which I say?'

Jesus' invitation flies in the face of modern evangelism. More often than not, sermons imply that Jesus is a personal Saviour to help people get out of trouble and danger. He is pictured as standing anxious and ready to assist all who will simply sign a permission slip for him to be a Saviour. But there is silence about his being a Master to be followed, a Lord to be obeyed. In Scripture the demand for following as a disciple is made plain at the outset. The narrow gate is at the *beginning* of the narrow way to everlasting life. It is not an after-thought added for more enthusiastic believers.

Indeed Jesus is 'a very present help in trouble' [*Psa. 46:1*] to all who trust him. However, he never gives saving help to any who will not follow him. For Christ simply to have told the ruler that he gave men heavenly riches and eternal life would have been to deceive him. The sinner must know that Jesus will not be a Saviour to any man who refuses to bow to him as Lord.

Christ knew nothing of the man-made, twentieth-century suggestion that taking Jesus as Lord is optional. For him it was no second step which is essential for great blessings but unnecessary for entering God's kingdom. The altered message of today has deceived men and women by convincing them that Jesus will gladly be a Saviour even to those who refuse to follow him as Lord. It simply is not the truth! Jesus' invitation to salvation is, 'Come, follow me.'

Practical acknowledgement of Jesus' lordship, yielding to his rule by following, is the very fibre of saving faith. It is only those who 'confess with the mouth the *Lord Jesus*' [*Rom.* 10:9, emphasis added] that shall be saved. Believing and obeying are such parallel ideas that the New Testament interchanges the words. 'He that believeth on the Son of God hath everlasting life: and he that obeyeth not the Son shall not see life; but the wrath of God abideth on him' [*John* 3:36]. Believing is obeying. Without obedience, you shall not see life! Unless you bow to Christ's sceptre, you will not receive the benefits of Christ's sacrifice. That is just what Jesus said to the ruler.

This fellow sincerely wanted eternal life and would have cheerfully invited Jesus into his heart for that gift. Jesus was not waiting for the man's invitation to enter his heart. Christ was offering the terms:

> I will give you eternal life if you come and follow me. You become my servant. Submit your mind to my teachings; for I am the Great Prophet. Bow your will to my commandments; for I am your King. Only on these terms do I offer any salvation or life.

If Jesus were satisfied to save the rich man because he made an intellectual admission that he was the Saviour, the New Testament would be a different book. First, the young man would have gone away happy. Had Jesus been willing to be the personal Saviour of one over whom he was not Lord, John could not have written, 'He that saith, I know him, and keepeth not his commandments, is a liar, and the truth is not in him' [*1 John* 2:4]. Were he to offer the rich ruler heavenly treasures without the stipulation that he must follow him, James could never have instructed us that 'Faith without works is dead' [*James* 2:20].

'Eternal life' and 'treasures in heaven' which the youth sought were only part of the salvation Jesus came to bring. It was predicted, 'He shall save his people from their *sins*' [*Matt.* 1:21, emphasis added]; not from their destruction or their eternal poverty apart from this matter of sin. Jesus demanded that the ruler submit to him as Lord. Then he would be delivered from sin's power. Faith is not the nod of a head to a series of facts. It is following Christ.

How strange such preaching would be to the ears of your people! They have been used to talking about accepting Jesus' saving help. But he also demands confession of his rule, obedience to his authority, worshipful submission to him as Lord. Your friends have come to think of following the Lord as 'frosting on the cake.' What would they think if you insisted, as Jesus did, that bowing to Christ as absolute monarch is an essential prerequisite of entering God's kingdom?

If you preach as plainly as Jesus did, you are likely to find many 'evangelicals' frowning at you. 'You are complicating the truth and condemning our teaching,' they will complain. The charge of preaching salvation by works will often be heard. 'Surely you can't think that the mass of evangelicals are wrong! At least they are not wrong enough for you to risk disunity. Be quiet about these things or you will stir up a storm.' There will be a subtle appeal to stifle the gospel for the sake of unity. Will you water down Jesus' doctrine of faith to suit evangelical tradition? Unity was never more expensive.

Someone may ask,

> Do you mean to suggest that raising your hand, going forward, and praying with the counsellor isn't valid? An evangelist told me that it was as simple as A, B, C.
> Accept God's free gift;
> Believe that Jesus is the Son if God who died for sinners;
> Confess your sinfulness.

Well, this wasn't enough for the young man in Mark 10. Jesus insisted that he repent and follow himself as Lord.

Our generation has heard much about Jesus. But here is a precept from his lips that lies buried and forgotten. Even the simple concept of faith is sadly distorted. Clearly it is imperative that we revive the genuine invitation of the Master and shout it from the housetops: 'O deceived generation, there is no life eternal unless you follow him. But he invites you to come in the posture of submission. Then he will give you life.'

Our Lord Jesus Christ was fully honest with the rich inquirer. He plainly asserted that following would involve a cross. 'Take up the cross,' that instrument of pain. 'In the world ye shall have tribulation' [*John* 16:33], the Master assured his disciples. The young ruler was informed at the beginning that obedience to Jesus would call for discomfort and sacrifice. In addition to turning away from the chief delights of his carnal lusts, he must also give up much that is legitimate as far as God's law is concerned. Friends would be lost. Anguished hours of self-examination and prayer were along the road. Discipleship is costly.

'Sit down first, and count the cost' [*Luke* 14:28], Jesus was saying to the convicted rich man.

I do not wish to trick you. I am not offering the end of worldly sorrows nor flowery beds of ease. I will not enlist you under false pretences. The road of following me is rough and steep. Stormy weather encompasses the entire course. There are many hills of difficulty and many valleys of humiliation for genuine Christians. So I set the symbol of a cross before you vividly to portray the difficulty and the personal demand made on my disciples. I want you to come. But I want you to weigh the cost as you follow.

Though unintentionally so, deceit marks many modern invitations to Christ. Audiences are reminded that they are sad, lonely, discouraged, and unsuccessful. Life is a great weight to them. Troubles encompass them. The future holds dark threats. Then sinners are invited to come to Christ, who will change all of that and put a smile on their faces. He is pictured as a cosmic psychologist who will patch up all problems in one session on the inquiry-room couch. There is no reminder of the discipline which Christ demands. No suggestion is given that following Jesus is sacrificial and painful.

It isn't surprising that many who 'go forward' to try the 'modern gospel' pill are never seen again. They react like a young military recruit. The recruiting sergeant told him about seeing the world, about honour and fortune and training. But nothing was said of early rising, forced marches, K.P. duty[1]. There was no mention of the blood, fire and terror of the battlefield. Sometimes the young 'convert', after a few days of professing Christ, wakes up to discover that troubles are compounded. The psychological honeymoon has ended so quickly. Thinking that he was duped by the dreamy promise of the evangelist, he is never seen again.

In total disregard of the transient nature of the 'convert's' experience, he is recorded as a statistic to prove the success of the latest evangelistic or missionary effort. He does not present himself for baptism or church membership. He does not teach Sunday School or even attend. He isn't serving in the church. He neither witnesses nor

---

1 'Kitchen police' or 'kitchen patrol' duty in the US military.

edifies the body of Christ. If the 'convert' has enhanced an evangelist's reputation, he has also given the poor pastor and church frustration and no end of headaches. As the independent evangelistic agencies reap joy, the church plunges into pitiful confusion and distress.

Integrity demands a more honest approach. The modern inquirer deserves to be treated as the young ruler. He must be told that the Lord to whom we are calling him will expect him to bear the cross. To impress hearts with the gravity of the decision before them, we would do well to say, 'Sit down and consider,' rather than 'Stand up and come forward.' 'Don't walk into this blindly. When you set your hand to this plough, you must not turn back. There is treasure in heaven. But it belongs to those who "take up the cross" on earth.'

Such preaching, though biblical, doesn't fit into the schedule of present-day evangelism. After the sermon, public indication of decision is on the programme. We can't disappoint all the Christians by sending sinners home to think about the weighty issues of eternity! When all the evening we have waited to see the climax of people visibly accepting Jesus, we cannot put such obstacles in the way of our expectations! Think what such measures would do to our campaign! Why, people might go away grieved!

There is no evidence that the rich youth ever trusted Christ and repented of sin. But he was honestly confronted with the gospel and its implications for his life. He was not tricked into a confession by the high-pressure sales techniques of modern personal workers. There was no subtle manipulation of him by psychological methods common to the salesman. When he went away, he really knew the full answer to his initial question.

5

Preaching Assurance of Acceptance with God

And he was sad at that saying, and went away grieved: for he had great possessions. [Mark 10:22]

Jesus did not address himself to the subject of assurance in this encounter with the ruler. But that is informative in itself. So many Christian workers feel compelled to do the Holy Spirit's work of giving assurance in their evangelism! It is all part of the ignorant assumption that when a man has 'come forward' he has come to Christ. Surely, when he repeats the counsellor's prayer with his lips, the sinner has earnestly called on God with his heart!

To perpetrate this delusion, a sentence is added to the 'salvation liturgy' which is not so much addressed to God as to the sinner who is repeating the prayer. 'Thank you for coming into my life and for hearing my prayer as you promised.' Then the personal worker is to open his Bible to John 3:16 etc., and replace the word 'world' with the sinner's name. Then the misguided counsellor is to assure the sinner with all the authority of God that he has been saved. A warning is added not to sin against God by ever doubting his salvation, for that would be to call God a liar.

This heretical and soul-destroying practice is the logical conclusion of a system that thinks little of God, preaches no law, calls for no repentance, waters down faith to 'accepting a gift', and never mentions bowing to Christ's rule or bearing a cross. The very practice of trying to argue men into assurance with a verse or two, and the ridiculous warning, 'Don't call God a liar' show that even 'accepting the gift' requires only an outward response and a verbal prayer. Though this is seldom intended, it is the distinct impression given to the 'converts'.

Orthodox churches often have their own version of man-given assurance. Here a communicant's class replaces the inquiry room, and catechism answers replace the repeated prayer. It is assumed that the routine answers given in a membership class are adequate proof of having trusted Christ. To question the conversion of the confirmed is unthinkable unless there is gross iniquity. Any doubts of the young communicant are swept aside by adults as a misunderstanding of the covenant. By inference, the young generation concludes that an intellectual assent to a strict set of doctrines guarantees their salvation. This system, too, ignores the necessity for an inward experience of grace. Though God, the Law, repentance and faith are all defined beautifully, they are left unapplied. An honest confrontation with the demands of Christ's Lordship—a cross to bear in this world—is bypassed.

Jesus Christ was not seeking to end the interview with the ruler making an overt response in doctrine or with the repetition of a prayer. He loved the man's soul and wanted it to be spiritually joined to its Maker by inward repentance and faith. No doubt traditional evangelical techniques would have given the rich man assurance before he left. And there would never be a question of his conversion. After all, he 'went forward' on the road before Jesus. He prayed the right prayer, asking for eternal life. In the inquiry room the ruler was evidently affected with grief. Perhaps he wept. Who would dare to 'call God a liar' by saying he wasn't saved? There was no gross sin in his life, or wrong doctrine whereby to question that he was a child of the covenant. But he wasn't! Men may be deeply affected by truth without being converted. Devils believe sound doctrine and tremble [*James* 2:19]. The ruler believed and was sad, but still lost.

There are tremendous implications in this passage for the doctrine of assurance. None of today's favourite signs of God's saving a man are valid. Repetition is needed here because of the myths entrenched in our evangelical world. The ruler went forward publicly but was not saved. He sincerely asked Jesus for eternal life but was not given that gift. He was visibly moved by the message of Christ but was not converted. He would have done well in a catechism class at that moment; for he obviously agreed with what our Lord said about himself. Yet he was as lost as ever.

Anyone who would give this lover of riches assurance would be fighting God. To tell him that his request for life had been granted because God always grants salvation to those who verbally ask would be a lie. It would contradict Jesus' word and destroy the man's soul by giving a false hope. To sweep aside his sadness by a vague appeal to his covenant position would be as deceitful. But just such false peace is being given to hundreds of men, women and children by pastors and missionaries.

Giving false assurance to sinners is a scriptural sign of a false prophet. 'From the prophet even unto the priest every one dealeth falsely. They have healed also the bruise of my people slightly, saying, Peace, peace; when there is no peace' [Jer. 6:14]. It is the Holy Spirit's work to assure the hearts of God's children. Thus, our forefathers would not have used the methods of assurance which are in vogue today.

As the Westminster Confession[1] so clearly states the biblical position on assurance, it is worthy of your careful attention:

> 1 Although hypocrites, and other unregenerate men, may vainly deceive themselves with false hopes and carnal presumptions of being in the favour of God and estate of salvation; which hope of theirs shall perish; yet such as truly believe in the Lord Jesus, and love him in sincerity,

[1] A similar statement is found in the London or Philadelphia Confessions of the Baptists.

endeavouring to walk in all good conscience before him, may in this life be certainly assured that they are in the state of grace, and may rejoice in the hope of the glory of God; which hope shall never make them ashamed.

2 This certainty is not a bare conjectural and probable persuasion, grounded upon a fallible hope; but an infallible assurance of faith, founded upon the divine truth of the promises of salvation, the inward evidence of those graces unto which these promises are made, the testimony of the Spirit of adoption witnessing with our spirits that we are the children of God: which Spirit is the earnest of our inheritance, whereby we are sealed to the day of redemption.

3 This infallible assurance doth not so belong to the essence of faith, but that a true believer may wait long, and conflict with many difficulties, before he be partaker of it: yet, being enabled *by the Spirit* to know the things which are freely given him of God, he may, without extraordinary revelation, in the right use of ordinary means, attain thereunto. And therefore it is the duty of everyone to give all diligence to make his calling and election sure; that thereby his heart may be enlarged in peace and joy in the Holy Ghost, in love and thankfulness to God, and in strength and cheerfulness in the duties of obedience, the proper fruits of this assurance: so far is it from inclining men to looseness.

4 True believers may have the assurance of their salva-

tion divers ways shaken, diminished, and intermitted; as, by negligence in preserving of it; by falling into some special sin, which woundeth the conscience, and grieveth the Spirit; by some sudden or vehement temptation; by God's withdrawing the light of his countenance, and suffering even such as fear him to walk in darkness, and to have no light: yet are they never utterly destitute of that seed of God, and life of faith, that love of Christ and the brethren, that sincerity of heart and conscience of duty, out of which, *by the operation of the Spirit*, this assurance may in due time be revived, and by the which, in the mean time, they are supported from utter despair.

Sometimes the honest thing to do is to send inquirers home grieved and counting the cost. The conditions of eternal life are not simply to come forward, confess sin and ask forgiveness. Unless a sinner turns from his sin and bows to Jesus the Lord, he cannot have eternal life. These requirements cannot be identified with any outward acts. Faith and repentance are the inward movement of mind, emotion and will. They cannot be measured by simple outward tests.

It is the Holy Spirit who must give assurance to Christians. 'The Spirit itself (not the personal worker himself) beareth witness with our spirit that we are the children of God' [*Rom.* 8:16]. 'Hereby we know that he abideth in us, by the Spirit which he hath given us' [*1 John* 3:24.]

God's Spirit gives this blessed confidence of sins forgiven to those who examine themselves in the light of God's Word. 'Examine yourselves whether ye be in the faith; prove your own selves' [2 *Cor.* 13:5]. 'If a man loves me, he will keep my words: and my Father will love him, and we will come unto him, and make our abode with him' [*John* 14:23].

The promises of the Bible respecting assurance are not given indiscriminately. They never lead men to expect that they can be in a state of acceptance with God without their also being renewed in a state of holiness. To the need of such a thorough moral change Jesus points the young ruler with the command, 'Sell whatsoever thou hast, and give to the poor . . . and come, take up the cross and follow me.' And the ruler's refusal to meet Christ on these terms at once excluded him from the promise, 'Thou shalt have treasure in heaven.'

Of course this does not mean that we must look for outward morality as a certain sign that a man has eternal life. The young ruler was exemplary from his youth in keeping the visible aspects of God's law. But it does teach us that self-examination must penetrate to the innermost chambers of the soul. Has grace bent the heart to glad submission to Christ's word? What motives move the will? What thoughts dominate the mind? What objects stir favourable emotions? Only when God is loved supremely and the spirit of the law kept has a man any reason to believe that he has been truly born of God.

Religious enthusiasm is also not a valid test of our acceptance with God. This young fellow would put many Christians to shame in his openly sincere desire to prepare for the world to come. His discipline in the search of purity was amazing. But he wasn't saved; for Christ did not hold his unqualified allegiance. Only when a person finds such dedication to Christ in his soul can he conclude that he is a disciple.

By the close of the conversation, the man who initiated it had correct information. Now his thinking was orthodox. That he had adopted Jesus' creed is evident from his sadness. Had he imagined that Christ's instructions were in error, he might have been angry, but not sad. The Master 'made good sense'. He agreed with the conclusions of the Lord. 'God is holy: I am covetous; the only way to inherit eternal life is to turn away from my money; if I am to have treasure in heaven, I must follow the Lord.' Yet correct knowledge was not enough. He must find in himself a proper heart response of obedience to gospel information if he is to conclude that he is a Christian. He dare not assume that the absence of heresy or immorality guaranteed his safety since he came from a covenant family. Positive evidence of devotion to Christ must be discovered for genuine assurance.

Nor is serious conviction a sign that a man has been converted. When he arrived at his home, the ruler could not sink into his plush bed and decide that all was well with his soul. The deep exercise of soul evidenced in sadness was no sign of favour with God. Because we are surrounded by cold hearts of stone, we are apt to judge that anyone who is deeply moved by the truth to an emotional expression has been saved. It is not so. The ruler was moved but unchanged. Proper grounds for assurance would be an inward delight in the gospel and an inward approval that effected outward transformation. This fellow had an aversion to the terms for receiving life, though he agreed intellectually to their wisdom and justice.

Few today seem to understand the Bible's doctrine of assurance. Few seem to appreciate the doubts of professing Christians who question whether they have been born again. They have no doubt that God will keep his promises but they wonder whether they have properly fulfilled the conditions for being heirs to those promises. There is no question that God will give eternal life to all who repent and believe. But they are discerning enough to know that walking an aisle and muttering a verbal prayer does not constitute faith. The Catechism's doctrine has raised valid questions concerning their personal experience of grace which cannot be brushed aside. They are asking a legitimate question, 'Have *we* believed and repented? Are *we* the recipients of God's grace?'

Since the human heart is 'deceitful above all things' [*Jer.* 17:9], this is a valid inquiry.

Since we read of self-deceived hypocrites like Judas, it is an imperative question. 'What must I do to be saved?' is an altogether different question from, 'How do I know that I've done it?' You can answer the first question confidently. Only the Spirit may answer the last with certainty.

How many souls have been led to vain confidence by a man-made, evangelistic formula? How many are sent home from evangelistic services with calm, who should have gone away as grieved and disturbed as the ruler? How many unsaved children have been given assurance by the teachers of Bible classes, so that they have ceased to seek God's salvation? When the rich ruler went home still given over to sin, there was at least a prick of conscience that made him uncomfortable in his rebellion. Perhaps he would trust Christ another day. But the dreadful false peace of today's salesmanship evangelism will kill conviction before it can do its God-intended work. It will stifle all search for God by a premature and humanly-manufactured assurance.

When Abraham attempted to hasten the arrival of an heir, he produced Ishmael, 'a wild man' [*Gen.* 16:12]. He used a fleshly procedure and secured a fleshly offspring. As God so plainly reminds us, 'They which are the children of the flesh, these are *not* the children of God.' [*Rom.* 9:8, emphasis added]. However much Abraham might declare to Ishmael that he was a beloved son,

God would disown him. Modern evangelism is filling the church with Ishmaels. Because of fleshly haste, evangelists produce 'converts' whom they call sons. But God will not own them. He is looking for Isaacs. When children are born through God-appointed techniques, then God will himself assure them that they are heirs to the promises.

Jesus' example as an evangelist condemns modern practice and doctrine. The interview terminated abruptly with the child of the flesh undeceived. The ruler was sad and went away grieved.

6

PREACHING WITH DEPENDENCE UPON GOD

And Jesus looked round about, and saith unto his disciples, How hardly shall they that have riches enter into the kingdom of God! And the disciples were astonished at his words. But Jesus answereth again, and saith unto them, Children, how hard is it for them that trust in riches to enter into the kingdom of God! It is easier for a camel to go through the eye of a needle, than for a rich man to enter into the kingdom of God. And they were astonished out of measure, saying among themselves, Who then can be saved? And Jesus looking upon them saith, With men it is impossible, but not with God: for with God all things are possible. [Mark 10:23-27]

Though he had come 'running', the greedy youth also 'went away grieved.' The most hopeful prospects often disappoint those of us who can only 'look on the outward appearance.' Though evangelists often see only the first signs of interest in the gospel, pastors who do not move on in a few days observe the sad scene of seekers turning away. Our Lord used this instance to instruct disciples who would often experience a similar 'let down.'

'How hard is it for them that trust in riches to enter into the kingdom of God!' Christ might just as easily have said, 'How hard is it for them that are angry to enter into the kingdom;' or 'It is easier for a camel to go through the eye of a needle, than for an adulterous man to enter the kingdom of God;' or 'How hard is it for disobedient children to enter the kingdom.' Jesus was simply using this specific sinner as an illustration of a general truth.

Our response could approximate to that of the disciples: 'They were astonished out of measure.' It is altogether an impossibility for a large animal to pass through the small eye of a needle. We must repeat the disciples' consternation, 'Who then can be saved?' The lesson is hard to accept. It quenches the fire of human hope. The gates of life seem to be slammed in the faces of humanity's throngs. Jesus' answer precludes any suggestion that he was using figurative language or hyperbole to say, 'It is difficult for a man to enter God's kingdom.' Jesus agreed with his disciples. Their tone of voice showed that they thought it beyond possibility for men to be saved. Jesus shook his head. 'You are right. You have not misunderstood my illustration,' the Lord was saying. 'With men it is impossible.'

But are evangelicals daunted or dismayed by our Master's astonishing statement on evangelism? On the contrary! They propose four easy steps to heaven. It's as simple as A, B, C. Just accept, believe and confess. A three-sentence prayer and you will be safe for eternity. Christ's statement alone should arrest the drift to simplicity and brevity in evangelism.

The Lord had told the ruler what he must do to have eternal life. He was informed that he could enter God's kingdom by repenting and believing. Now Jesus was flatly telling his disciples that he had demanded the impossible! It was impossible for the rich youth to sell all and follow. The ruler was a slave to Satan. His mind was perverted, his emotions twisted, his will enslaved. He could not obey the gospel commands to repent and believe. The very constitution of his nature opposed such action.

Jeremiah eloquently established the impossibility of men turning from sin to follow the Lord. 'Can the Ethiopian change his skin, or the leopard his spots? then may ye also do good, that are accustomed to do evil' [*Jer.* 13:23]. Answers to the rhetorical quiz are plain. Black men cannot make themselves white. Leopards cannot discard their spots at will. 'Well then,' says the prophet, 'neither have you habitual sinners any capacity to turn to doing good.'

The ruler was commanded to repent, but he had no native ability to repent. There was no pure, or even neutral, element of his character to respond favourably to this appeal of Christ. Like the rest of humanity, 'every imagination of the thoughts of his heart was only evil continually' [*Gen.* 6:5]. There was no spark of goodness in him to influence his will to accept Christ's invitation. He was 'dead in trespasses and sins' [*Eph.* 2:1]. Not half alive, or dangerously sick, but dead.

Even while Jesus sincerely and compassionately said, 'Come, follow me,' he knew very well that 'No man can come to me except the Father which hath sent me draw him' [*John* 6:44]. So incapable was this sinner of even a step of faith, that he must be born again to enter God's kingdom. Nor would his will ever select a new birth for himself. All those who ever believed on Jesus 'were born, not of the will of men, but of God' [*John* 1:13]. This hopelessly covetous ruler would be no exception. 'With men it is impossible.'

Modern evangelism has been developed with the supposition that God has already done what he can to save man. He is commonly pictured as standing idly by simply to observe what sinners will decide to do with his Son and his salvation. God is treated as if his Spirit were not in the world to convict of sin, reveal Christ, and regenerate sinners. Now sinners must exercise the power of their natural wills. One popular handbook for evangelizing children has been so crass as to say, 'We must get the child to accept salvation . . . It is not enough to tell the child that he should accept Christ, we must get him to do it then and there.'[1] Any persuasive salesmanship calculated to release the latent power of the human will may be used.

---

1 *A Handbook on Child Evangelism*, by J. Irvin Overholtzer, published by International Child Evangelism Fellowship, Grand Rapids, Michigan, USA.

There can be no question that receiving Jesus Christ is an act of the human will. But how does that will come to trust the Saviour? Every man is born with an aversion to the truth, a hatred of God, and a love of independence from his law. The will, acting in concert with the mind and emotions, is certain to refuse God's truth, spurn reconciliation with the Maker, and laugh at submission to his commands. How is a will to choose an entirely new direction for itself? How can the youth sell all and follow Christ obediently? His entire being cries out against such a decision. Modern evangelism blindly continues to assume that men have a native ability to repent and believe. 'With men it is impossible.'

'Who then can be saved?' is still a pertinent question. And Jesus gives a clear, positive response, 'With God all things are possible.' Though no man can find in himself the necessary resolve and ability to repent and believe, God can so change a sinner's heart that he will sell all and follow Christ. The ruler's will could not drag him into the kingdom. Nor could his intelligence and emotions. But God could give him a new heart. 'A new heart also will I give you, and a new spirit will I put within you' [*Ezek.* 36:26], was God's promise. Only as God performed a work of re-creation upon his character could the youth repent and believe.

Faith is the act of a heart quickened by the sovereign power of God.

> For by grace are ye saved through faith; and that not
> of yourselves: it is the gift of God: not if works lest any
> man should boast. For we are his workmanship, created
> in Christ Jesus unto good works. [*Eph.* 2:8-10]

As God created a new spirit in the rich man, he could follow Christ. Though following was his responsibility, he
never would choose to do so unless the Lord gave him a
new inclination, that is, unless God in his mercy gave the
youth a new heart. Faith is the result of regeneration by
God's Spirit.

Repentance, too, is the act of a man who has received
the gift of life. Since this is true, repentance itself may
be said to be a gift of God. 'God has exalted Jesus with
his right hand to be a Prince and a Saviour, for to give
repentance to Israel and forgiveness of sins' [*Acts* 5:31].
The ruler would receive forgiveness of sins only if he repented. But repentance itself is a gift from the Saviour.
For the sinner to exercise repentance, a sovereign Lord
must take away the stony heart and replace it with a heart
of flesh.

The young man had asked, 'What shall I do?' Jesus
told him plainly to sell all and follow. When the answer
was given, he saw that he couldn't fulfil the conditions of
receiving eternal life. Not that Jesus prevented him from
complying! The Lord urged him to do it. Not that any
other force outside of himself hindered his repenting and
believing! But his own evil heart made it impossible. As

soon ask an elephant to fly as ask a covetous man to 'sell whatsoever thou hast and give to the poor.' As soon urge a starved lion to spare the tender lambs of an available flock and rather eat spinach. 'He was sad at the saying.' He just could not do it.

Jesus turned to his disciples and said, 'That's it. That is just the point. It is impossible for him to do it. But not so for God; with God all things are possible.' The God of all power can transform the basic nature of his creatures. He made them as a potter moulds a vase. He alone can make them anew in the image of his Son. He must so alter them that they will repent and believe. 'Marvel not that I say unto you, you must be born again' [*John* 3:7]. This casts sinners wholly upon God's power and grace. They must seek the Lord for salvation. Their only hope is to call on God to do for them what they cannot do for themselves.

Implications of our Saviour's lesson are many. He had been telling a dead man to breathe and walk. The ruler was dead in trespasses and sins. Yet Jesus commanded him to 'come forth' from the tomb of greed. There was no moral life in his limbs, yet Christ insisted that the sinner walk away from riches to serve the Messiah. Today's gospel preaching must make similar demands.

Though it is proper to reason with men, persuade men, beseech men, there will be no response unless God in his grace attends with enabling power the words we speak. Our evangelism must be based upon a dependence on the

Lord. Our hope of results must be in him, not in man's will or in any other faculty of our hearer. But it pleases God to raise dead sinners through the foolishness of gospel preaching.

Some object that such a view will stifle evangelism. It did not stifle our Lord. But why preach to the dead? When Jesus stood at the tomb of Lazarus, and cried, 'Lazarus, come forth' [*John* 11:43], you might have made a similar complaint. Why speak to the dead? How could the lifeless corpse obey the command? Would you invent the doctrine that all of Lazarus had died but his will? Yes, that would do! He was really dead, except that the will never dies. So when Jesus says, 'Come forth,' the will of Lazarus can obey. Let's learn the secret of persuading the wills of dead men and medical science will marvel at our power to raise the dead.

How absurd to suggest that the free will of Lazarus decided to obey Christ, and that was how the dead man was revived! When he walked out of the tomb in grave clothes, Lazarus had indeed exercised his will in obeying Jesus' voice. But that could be done only as God quickened the whole man to life (ears to hear, mind to understand, will to obey at the call). God gave him a new life! His response to Jesus was the result and evidence of God's sovereign act of resurrection.

When Jesus spoke to the rich ruler, he was speaking to a dead man whose will was as dead as his intellect and feelings - dead toward God and alive toward sin. Jesus commanded that he 'come.' Only as God raised him from the dead would he respond. 'Even when we were dead in sins, God hath quickened us together with Christ' [*Eph.* 2:5]. This is resurrection language. With the ruler it was impossible, but not with our supernatural God.

We are called to preach to dead bones [*Ezek.* 37]. As Ezekiel of old, we are placed in the valley of this world which is filled with the parched bones of dead sinners. And we are told, 'Prophesy upon these bones' [verse 4]. It is God's purpose to raise dead sinners to life through our preaching. The bones are 'very dry'. There isn't even the sinew of free will upon them. But as God breathes, they will live and become 'an exceeding great army' following the Lamb - to the praise of the glory of his mighty grace.

This awareness will focus our primary attention upon humble prayer for God's saving power to attend us. Our confidence will not rest upon organizational unity or psychological techniques. Seeing the desperate plight of the bones and the hopelessness of all techniques and schemes of men, we shall be compelled carefully and plainly to prophesy just what we are told. Sinners, seeing their hopeless condition, will be forced to cast themselves on the Lord rather than rest on a personal act. No congress will bring flesh upon these bones. No merger of mission societies will raise up the army. No four easy steps in the hands of super-organized salesmen will make sinners live again. Only God, sovereignly working through a faithful messenger, can raise the dead to life.

Paul's advice to the young preacher Timothy will teach us that the only hope for the preacher or for the sinner is in God. Yet this is a great hope:

> 'The servant of the Lord must not strive; but be gentle unto all men, apt to teach, patient, in meekness instructing those that oppose themselves; *if God peradventure will give them repentance* to the acknowledging of the truth; and that they may recover themselves out of the snare of the devil, who are taken captive by him at his will' [2 *Tim.* 2:24-26, emphasis added].

Preachers are fenced into only one hope of success—'If God gives repentance' to their hearers. Oratory will not convince rebels. Clever devices will not reverse the steps of rich, young sinners. Careful preparation and energetic delivery of precise theology can do nothing in themselves. But 'if God' attends biblical messages and means, the dead will rise.

Sinners are boxed in to only one hope for recovering themselves from the iron grasp of the devil. It is, 'if God will give them repentance.' Far from this box extinguishing all hope, it has an exceeding broad hope. 'If God will give' is an infinitely brighter expectation than 'If man will get'. With 'If God' before him, a sinner may cry to God for his omnipotent mercy to save a helpless wretch.

Will being closed up to the power of God stifle evangelism? No! it will prompt the most needed activity of the hour—more prayer! Then it will send out preachers in confident zeal that the God who still raises the dead goes with them. And it will send sinners to their knees beseeching God to give salvation.

CONCLUSION

Differences between much of today's preaching and that of Jesus are not petty; they are enormous. The chief errors are not in emphasis or approach but in the heart of the gospel message. Were there a deficiency in one of the areas mentioned in these pages, it would be serious. But to ignore all—the attributes of God, the holy law of God, repentance, a call to bow to the enthroned Christ, as well as a perversion of assurance—is the most deadly mistake. There are no more crucial truths than these in Scripture.

Incredulity may grip you. Can so many evangelicals be so wrong? Can it be true that Christian people are misleading the souls of men in regard to salvation? Is it really all that bad? Look at the evangelistic missions with all their folk rock and other gimmicks. Evaluate the teachings of the Bible schools, the evangelical literature, the tactics of organizations working with young people. Examine them in the light of Jesus' preaching, and you will have to agree—the church is far from the New Testament message. Oh, and don't forget to look at your own preaching and teaching.

All are not in error, but great hosts are. All have not perverted the gospel to the same degree, but many are terribly far from the truth. All those who 'make decisions' are not deceived, but great numbers are. Above all, few care to recover the gospel message. Most assume that evangelical tradition embodies it. Great multitudes never carefully weigh their habits in the light of Scripture.

Certainly many evangelicals who practise the evangelistic evils which have been mentioned are sincerely seeking to serve Christ. Many have an experience that surpasses their understanding. And these errors do not negate in their minds other basic truths of God's Word. But sincerity and genuine conversion are not the only qualifications necessary for the work of an evangelist. An ability to convey the biblical gospel is essential.

Since evangelicals are honestly asking why God has not attended their giant projects with his power, it is time to re-examine the content of the gospel most popularly preached. We must plunge beneath the superficial reports on methods and unity to focus attention on the foundational issue—the doctrine fostered by our evangelism and missions. Surely no issue can supersede the necessity of preaching the truth Christ delivered to his disciples!

Needed most of all, then, is the demolition of the dreadful trend that sees the gospel as simply a few facts. True evangelism preaches the whole counsel of God with explanation and application to sinners. Remember our Lord's dealings with the young ruler. Let them guide your message and methods. Don't sell this truth for unity or any other product. The gospel of our Lord Jesus Christ is a pearl worthy to be purchased at the cost of all else. Rise above deadening evangelical tradition and 'earnestly contend for the faith which was once delivered unto the saints' [*Jude* 3].

Soli Deo Gloria.

Select bibliography for further study

EVANGELISM
The Christian's Great Interest, William Guthrie
A Sure Guide to Heaven, Joseph Alleine
The Invitation System, Iain H. Murray

ATTRIBUTES OF GOD
Evangelism and the Sovereignty of God, James I. Packer
The Attributes of God, Arthur W. Pink

REGENERATION, REPENTANCE, AND FAITH
Redemption Accomplished and Applied, John Murray

ASSURANCE
Heaven on Earth, Thomas Brooks
Distinguishing Traits of True Christian Character, Gardiner Spring
The Religious Affections, Jonathan Edwards

THEOLOGY UNDERLYING EVANGELISM
Introduction to John Owen's *Death of Death*, James I. Packer
The Forgotten Spurgeon, Iain H. Murray
The Bondage of the Will, Martin Luther

Other Books by Walter Chantry

Habakkuk: A Wrestler with God
978 0 85151 995 1, 112 pages, paperback.

David, Man of Prayer, Man of War
978 0 85151 953 1, 304 pages, clothbound.

Signs of the Apostles
978 0 85151 175 7, 160 pages, paperback.

The Shadow of the Cross
978 0 85151 331 7, 80 pages, paperback.

God's Righteous Kingdom
978 0 85151 310 2, 160 pages, paperback.

Praises for the King of Kings
978 0 85151 587 8, 120 pages, paperback.

Call the Sabbath a Delight
978 0 85151 588 5, 120 pages, paperback.

For more information about our publications, or to
order, please visit our website.

THE BANNER OF TRUTH TRUST

3 Murrayfield Road,   P O Box 621, Carlisle,
Edinburgh EH12 6EL   PA 17013,
UK   USA
www.banneroftruth.co.uk